There's No Such Thing As A Perfect Wedding

True Wedding Tales, Odd, Funny and Disastrous

Margaret G. Bigger

Illustrated by Tim Rickard

DOWN HOME **Down Home Press**   **Asheboro, N.C**

ISBN 1-878086-04-9

Library of Congress Catalog Card Number 91-071001

Printed in the United States of America

Cover design by Tim Rickard
Illustrations by Tim Rickard
Book design by Elizabeth House

Down Home Press
P.O. Box 4126
Asheboro, N.C. 27204

Introduction

There is no such thing as a perfect wedding, except in a storybook – and this is no such book.

True wedding tales are favorite topics among ministers, church organists and florists, but the ones passed down for generations are obviously the most unforgettable, particularly for the hapless brunt of family chuckles.

All unusual occurrences at, before and after a marriage ceremony are not accidental. Some are not humorous, merely odd. Others are deliberate attempts to be different, such as the wedding at which the bride insisted that they play her favorite popular song, *Send in the Clowns*. That theme could be appropriate for quite a few of the occasions described in this collection of tales.

Brides' families, take notice. There are many implied tips here, suggesting what not to do.

You just might discover that, at most nuptials, there are not only something borrowed and something blue, but something slightly crazy, too.

Contents

There's No
Such Thing
As A Perfect Wedding

Preliminaries

Not all odd happenings occur during the ceremony. Sometimes the snafus, silliness and sagas begin before the wedding day.

All the groom's family were gathering in an Illinois motel, far from home. It was Friday before the Saturday wedding, and the groom had gone to get the blood test and marriage license in the bride's hometown. When he returned, his folks knew immediately that something was seriously wrong. It was. He had failed the blood test and couldn't get a license!

The groom was depressed; his parents, humiliated; his in-laws, horrified. More family was coming in, and there could be no wedding! His sister reminded everyone of her brother's shyness with girls and noted that the bride-to-be was only the second one he had ever dated. That consoled no one. The bride's reaction to the news, they heard, was to get into the bathtub and fill it with her tears. Nobody could get her out.

Late that afternoon, there came a furious knock on the door of the motel room where they were brooding. When they opened it, a huge woman, the mother of the bride, burst in, grabbed her daughter's boyfriend and took him away with her.

As it was too late to cancel the rehearsal dinner, the family glumly attended. It was, of course, an awkward occasion. About 8:30 p.m., the honorees arrived, escorted by the bride's mother. Although the bride, who had been retrieved from the bathtub "looked a wreck," the groom had a relieved expression. His mother-in-law-to-be was all smiles. Someone had inadvertently mixed up the blood samples the first time. When she had taken him to the hospital for a re-test, he had passed.

Loud music attracted the ire of apartment dwellers near the site of the bachelor party. It was quite late, for the party had begun after the rehearsal dinner. A police car responded to the neighbors' calls. Unfortunately, a certain party-goer tends to talk ugly when drunk, and he was the first to exchange words with the officer. The confrontation became louder than the music.

To find out what was going on, the groom's father stepped out of the apartment. In his hand was a drink. The next thing he knew, both hands were in handcuffs, and he, too, was arrested. The groom came out. He was put in the squad car with his father. His brother drove up about that time. A photographer by trade, he saw the humor of the situation and got out his camera. While he was snapping photos of his sibling's and father's predicament, the fed-up policeman arrested him for obstructing justice.

The mother-of-the-groom soon got a call from her husband at the police station. "What must I do?" she asked.

"I don't know," he replied. "I've never been in jail before."

What she did was to contact a lawyer, take up a cash collection for bail and wake up the father-of-the-bride (who never takes a drink, by the way) to ask him to take her to the station.

At approximately 2:00 a.m., they arrived, cash in hand. Bail had been set for the "obstructor of justice," but the groom and his father were required to stay in the "drunk tank" until 6:00 a.m. Five hours and a catnap later, they all appeared at the church on time and in place.

Their car screeched in front of the bride-to-be's house not long before midnight. Bachelor-party-goers dragged the howling groom from the car. All he had on were his skivvies. Luckily, he had worn his plaid boxer shorts that night. Everyone knows that plaids and stripes don't go together, but his buddies had shaved his hairy legs in stripes anyway.

To a huge tree in his fiancee's yard, the guys chained and handcuffed him. They threw the key in the driveway and roared off. In the groom's family's yard, they piled his clothes next to a railroad flare and rang the doorbell. Guilt must have gotten to some of them,

4

though, for they returned to the home of the bride to yell, "The key is in the driveway."

By that time, several neighbors who had been aroused by the noise were milling around the yard, trying to figure out what to do for the shackled groom and furious bride. The bride called the police.

The groom, who refused to give his name to an amused reporter, was freed from the cuffs at the city jail. "By Saturday," warned the officer, "you may wish you were on that tree."

To this day, a silver anniversary later, the bride is still angry about the incident. The instigator of the plot recalls that the inspiration came from yet another tale: the one about the bunch of so-called friends who got the groom stone drunk, striped him naked, dumped him in a gunny sack, took him to the bride's front porch and rang the doorbell. They thought their trick was tame.

As the bride's mother turned out of the Kroger parking lot, she heard a sickening "kerplop." The lovely three-tier custom made wedding cake she had just picked up had fallen off the back seat and smashed on the floor. Tearfully, she raced back to the grocery to tell her sad tale to the bakery manager. It was 9:00 a.m. The wedding would be at noon.

"Everyone in the store helped out," remembered the cake-designer. The manager sent clerks to run her cash register and handle customers. Others pitched in to mix, bake and ice another just-as-beautiful cake.

Five minutes before noon, someone stopped by to pick up the beflowered masterpiece, a gift to the unknown bride and groom.

His office was "spic and span," an unusual state for the chambers he shared with another superior court judge.

"There's going to be a wedding here today," their secretary said in explanation.

"Who's going to perform it?" he wanted to know. She nodded toward the other judge's chambers. "He's got his Episcopal prayer book and is all ready."

He stepped into his fellow-judge's quarters and asked in a serious tone, "On what authority are you going to conduct this wedding?"

"As a judge."

"Perhaps you should look up the law. In this state, only a justice of the peace has that power. Better find an Episcopal priest."

A middle-aged woman tells of a young man of her acquaintance who bought marriage licenses twice in one week with two different women.

"Did you really buy two licenses?" she asked him incredulously.

"Yes, I'm getting married this Saturday. But I haven't decided to which one yet."

A Pennsylvania bride called her minister after the rehearsal. For this debutante, the church seemed only an incidental part of the society wedding of the year. Thus, the minister was surprised by her phone call.

"Reverend, do I have to promise to obey him?" she asked plaintively.

"No," he replied. "You have to do something far more difficult."

"What?"

"Love him."

Two women in Greenwood, Mississippi, had been asked to decorate for the wedding of a friend's daughter. Church staffers had mentioned that a youth revival was taking place that weekend, and a banner would be hanging over the choir loft behind the pulpit. The volunteers had planned to hang greenery around the banner and place flowers and candles beneath it. That is, until they saw the banner. It read: "He is able."

More excited than her daughter, the mother-of-the-bride rushed off to the church early to get flowers pinned prettily into her hair. The bride's sister had already departed from their country home to put on her bridesmaid's dress at the church.

The bride had been left behind with no car. Her only choice was to call a cab.

Some men have odd ways of "popping the question."

"I love you Pam. Will you marry me?" was on the banner trailing a private plane. It circled a football stadium four times. Pam reportedly said yes.

Her boyfriend took her for a ride in his 1926 roadster. They were approaching a bridge over a creek, when suddenly, he lurched the car over to one side, drove to the water's edge, and kept going until the car halted in the middle of the moving water. "We're going to stay here until you say 'yes' to marrying me," the young man declared.

"I would have said 'yes' on dry land," she replied.

This groom proposed with a big rock. Only it wasn't a diamond. It was a huge white-washed rock in front of a high school on his girlfriend's route to work. He red-painted "Lisa marry me" and a heart on it. On a smaller rock, he wrote "hee hee," his peculiar way of laughing. On an even smaller rock, he put his initials. It took Lisa two days and several trips by the school to notice his message.

The South Carolina college student stood before his theater and speech class. His final exam began like this: "Today I would like to pay tribute to someone who is very dear to me."

The other students sat silently, when he finished his talk. His girlfriend, who had attended the class to give him moral support, thought a moment before saying "yes" to his public proposal. Silence became applause and laughter. The student got an "A" and a bride.

We promised our parents that we would notify them as soon as I got the ring, so that they could start telling their friends. My husband-to-be presented the diamond at a night club near Chapel Hill, where I was in college. But when we asked directions to a public telephone, we were each pointed to the appropriate restroom. We sought another nearby and found one in the motel parking lot next door. We called my mother first. "Where are you?" she wanted to know.

"We're at a mo...t..th'...phone booth...uh...next to the club," I stammered, hot with fear. In the '50s, to tell your mother you were in a motel with a boyfriend was a SIN.

Some experiences are so memorable that they have been re-told generation after generation within a family. Here are two such stories.

An elderly lady who grew up on Roanoke Island, North Carolina, will never forget being awakened at 3:00 a.m. to don a

8

flower girl's dress. Sleepily, she, as a youngster, had to perform her part in a family wedding an hour later.

Why were fashionable weddings held at 4:00 or 5:00 a.m.?

"Because anyone in the early 1900s who could afford a honeymoon took the Hattie Creef, the only public transportation from the island to the Mainland," she explained.

The little steamboat, captained by her father, departed Manteo daily at 6:00 a.m.

An ensign in the Argentine navy at the turn of the century was to be an usher in a friend's wedding. For his gift to the couple, he selected an elegant crystal bowl.

But, alas, he dropped it while he was still in the store, and it broke. The shopkeeper, of course, made him pay for that one, and he did not have the money for another.

Not dejected for long, the young Argentine officer returned to his family's home with a plan. He instructed the maid to wrap the gift anyway and summoned the butler to deliver it. To the butler, he said in Spanish, "Ring the doorbell, and when someone opens it, drop the package."

At the reception, everyone was talking about the cute joke played by the ensign. The couple's family thought it was hilarious that he would give a broken crystal bowl with each piece wrapped individually.

Delayed Ceremony

To begin a marriage ceremony even five minutes late advertises that something is amiss. But some delays have been considerably longer.

It was in the late '30s. A minister's daughter simply could not decide whether she wanted to marry her fiance or not. Her "intended" had come to her hometown from his several-hundred-miles-away home, so her father could perform the service. After he arrived, she made up her mind that they should call it off.

The dejected, would-be bridegroom got back on a bus and rode home. As soon as he got there, the capricious girl was calling to say she really did want to marry him after all. Back to the bus station he trekked to catch the next motor coach to her town.

At 2:00 a.m., they were side-by-side in the bride's living room to be joined in holy matrimony.

"I can't marry you at this indecent hour!" exclaimed the father. He whirled around, strode to the clock and turned back the hands. "Dearly beloved, we are gathered here..."

A bride in a 1950s wedding was nearly an hour late. Oh, she was at the church but nowhere near the aisle. The organist played hymn after hymn. Bridesmaids stood first on one dyed satin shoe and then another. Ushers paced. A bridesmaid checked the bride's dressing room and summoned her own mother from the congregation to help.

The problem: The mother-of-the-bride had not finished making the wedding gown. A few parts were missing including the zipper. There was no long white zipper handy at the church, so the

11

bridesmaid's mother sewed the bride into her dress, while the forgetful mother fretted.

This 1980s wedding was delayed by a human traffic jam. More people had been invited to the wedding than the church could seat. For 45 minutes, ushers tried to figure our what to do with them all. Then the procession took longer than most Protestant ceremonies. There were 43 participants. That included not only a flower girl and ring bearer but junior bridesmaids and a "junior bridegroom" (yes, "bridegroom" not "groomsman") plus several soloists and two ministers. To the consternation of one minister, the other conducted communion. The entire process took so long that the children sat down to rest.

In this situation, the sister of the bride had eloped, so all the family's dreams had been put into this occasion. The mother-of-the-bride even added a new idea. The invitation read: "(her name) and (her late husband's name) in spirit cordially invite you to the wedding of their daughter."

In a small Virginia town, the bank president's secretary's wedding was one of the biggest social events of the season. Everyone who was "anyone" was in the First Presbyterian Church – except the minister. The ushers were in front and the bridesmaids were on their way down the aisle when someone called the minister's house to urge him to hurry. No one was home! Frantically, someone called a Baptist preacher. Hot and sweaty, he gasped that he had been mowing his lawn. So the talk of the town that summer was of the slightly-stinky Baptist who pinch-hit for the absent-minded Presbyterian.

In the early '70s, a bride dreamed of a wedding in her backyard garden. During premarital counseling, the preacher asked if she had planned what to do if it rained.

"No! It will be in our backyard," she declared.

Her wedding day dawned brightly but clouded just before the mid-afternoon ceremony. Sprinkles of rain fell on the pretty trellis and the rows of chairs.

"We'll wait awhile," determined the bride, whose house was like a sardine can packed with guests with no place to sit.

Indeed, the sun eventually did lighten the backyard and the spirits, and out people went to dry off everything. But surprise! More sprinkles. Only the bride ignored them. Guests hung back under the eaves or beneath umbrellas in the background, while the mothers were seated in their designated seats and the wedding party took their places. The bride refused to stand beneath a golf umbrella offered by the preacher.

That was more than frustrating for him, for his robe had velvet trim which could be ruined. He left off the robe and married them in his new suit, which, incidentally, was never the same after that. As he went through the service from the wedding book, there would be periodic pauses, so that he could peel the wet pages apart. Yet, despite his unpleasant feelings while soaking in the rain, he could hardly keep a straight face when glancing at the groom's mother. Her highly-teased hair was drooping down and down into a helmet around her head.

The preacher made a slight change in the vows, which he required the couple to repeat after him: "in sickness and in health, in sunshine and in rain."

The 35-year-old bride had pre-planned her wedding several months ahead but neglected a few details. The day before the ceremony, she asked the minister where she could buy some little napkins with his and her names on them. The night of the rehearsal, the minister wanted to know who was the maid-of-honor.

"I haven't decided yet," replied the bride. "Who would like to do that?" she asked her five attendants.

One raised her hand. "I've never been one. I'd like that."

At the appointed time, the wedding party was ready, but the bride's mother was not. She was not even there. For an hour, they awaited her arrival. When she came in, her hair was in curlers.

13

While someone was brushing out the mother's hair, the maid-of-honor asked the minister if she could sing a solo. Fine, if the organist knew the hymn. The organist had already played most of the hymnbook and was to play at another wedding in another church less than an hour from then, but she graciously agreed.

After that, there was one more delay. The ushers came in as planned. But the bridesmaids did not. When they finally took their places, it was not at all in the order which had been rehearsed. Later, the cause of the confusion was revealed. The other bridesmaids were jealous that the maid-of-honor also got to sing. They said it wasn't fair for her to do both and argued over who would take her place.

Neither the priest nor the groom nor the best man came out on cue. The organist played the wedding march over and over. The bride and her escort made their way to the front, and still they did not appear. Louder and louder, the organist played to jar the errant chit-chatters to attention. At last, she gave up, left the organ bench, clonked her high heels along the wooden aisle to the door, opened it and – to the amusement of the guests and the embarrassment of the bride – summoned the sheepish threesome.

Around a backyard pool in the fine suburban neighborhood of a Southern city, the guests gathered to see their friends united in marriage. But alas, the groom's britches were too tight. Several sizes too small, in fact. He must go all the way into town to exchange them at the rental store. Some two hours later, the ceremony began.

Thirty-five minutes after the delay was announced, the youthful organist had played every piece she knew at least twice. The minister told her to take a break, because the groom still was not ready. He had forgotten to pick up the ring from a jewelry store. On a Saturday afternoon in that Northern city in the '50s, jewelry stores were closed. Hard as the minister tried to convince him to substitute someone else's ring, the young man insisted on calling the shopkeeper to meet him downtown and give him the right one. One hour and a half later, the service resumed.

Can you imagine the embarrassment of having to call all 75 to 80 guests to come to your wedding on Monday instead of Saturday because you forgot to get the marriage license? On Friday, the couple (who were each marrying for the second time) realized their mistake. Florida had a waiting period, so they had no choice.

Friends held a bachelor party at a Canadian strip joint for an Italian immigrant who came to Detroit to get married. But when the group tried to cross the border to get back to Detroit, immigration officials would not let the bridegroom return. The trip had violated his visa.

The next day, his wedding day, he was caught trying to cross the border hidden in a trunk. Meanwhile, guests waited hours at the church for him to arrive. Finally, the wedding party piled into a limousine and took off for Canada. That night the couple were re-united, but despite the presence of a priest, not united in holy matrimony. They had no Canadian marriage license.

In the 1830s, a young girl in Carteret County, North Carolina, fell in love with the tutor her father had brought in from New England to educate his children. But the father did not want his daughter to leave the family, because she, as the oldest, was needed to care for the younger children. The tutor was sent away.

Over the years, the tutor sent love letters, but the father had them intercepted at the Beaufort post office. The young girl grew to womanhood but never married. Her sweetheart moved west and eventually became Chief Supreme Court Justice in the Arizona Territory.

Many years later, the postmaster, before his death, confessed his part in the deception. And so, in 1885, when her long-lost tutor wrote the town's postmaster to inquire about her, she responded herself. On May 20, 1886, they were married in Carteret County. On June 14, 1886, she died of consumption in the arms of her beloved.

Society pages were full of the preliminaries of this wedding. Both prominent families had made all the proper preparations. But the groom's fraternity brothers disapproved of the match. Two hours before the ceremony, they kidnapped the guy and took him out of state. They sent two ushers to the service to announce that there would be no wedding.

Both sets of parents were furious. The bride's father, an attorney, shouted about a lawsuit. But nothing they could do would bring him back.

The couple eventually were married, but not to each other.

One fiance reportedly promised his girlfriend that he would marry her the next time it snowed in their city. They lived in Miami.

Twenty years later, a freak snowstorm hit the South Florida metropolis. When the national press covered the extraordinary weather, they also announced the wedding. Before nightfall, the middle-aged bride-to-be had cashed in on his promise.

Not even a serious accident delayed this wedding. The groom in a leg cast was rushed from the hospital to the church, because his future mother-in-law declared, "We've spent too much on this wedding for it not to go on."

When this groom had an emergency appendectomy, the wedding was postponed, but the reception was not. "We had all the food, so everyone went and ate it." explained the bride's mother.

16

The day before his impending second marriage, the groom discovered that his first wife, whom he thought he divorced eight years before, had never completed the divorce papers. He and the ushers returned their rented tuxedos, and he took off for Chicago to straighten out his legal problems. At last report, the bride and her attendants were saving their dresses for future use.

When the florist returned to the church to pick up the rented items two hours after the scheduled wedding, family members were still milling around. The marriage license had been left behind in another town, and someone had gone to retrieve it.

Where the bride's family had found the organist, no one knew. Her performance was painful, to say the least.

At last, the prelude was over, and she fumbled through the processional, while the mothers were being seated.

Meanwhile, the groom was turning white. Fortunately, he was standing on the back porch of the church, for he leaned over and lost his lunch.

The minister began comforting him and sent the best man to notify the wedding director. Seeing the positive side of the situation, he called to the messenger: "Tell the organist to keep playing. She needs the practice."

18

Unusual Settings

Most ceremonies are held in a church, synagogue, home or justice of the peace office. But many couples choose a more memorable setting.

Cold was the March wind when two members of the American Coaster Enthusiasts (ACE) Club prepared to say their vows atop a roller coaster at Carowinds amusement park.

The groom had told his sweetheart of his love in a Canadian coaster car. Later, his proposal had been posted on a Carowinds marquee.

Watching his bride approach the Carowinds car in her long white gown and fur wrap, the groom did jumping jacks. A Charlotte radio personality, who was broadcasting live, made a crack about the groom getting "cold feet." The wedding couple climbed into the front of the car, while the minister settled on the second seat. Others scrambled into the rest of that train and an adjacent one.

Both trains rattled to the 85-foot apex, as wedding music played from a machine below. The Church of Christ minister, an ACE member who had come all the way from Pennsylvania, performed the ceremony. Following the nuptial kiss, the music was drowned out by screams.

Those who owned the cabin (which they termed a "shack") could not imagine why a distant relative wanted to be married there. True, there was a small farm pond nearby which could have been a picturesque, pastoral setting. But the bride did not choose to have it pondside. No, her service would be at one side of the cabin, and she would come down the crude wooden steps from the front door in her traditional white wedding gown. Her bridesmaids, wearing hand-made pink silk gowns, and the female guests in their finest outfits would walk in high heels through the reddish dirt to their places.

That summer afternoon in the 1970s was unusually hot. Perspiration glistened on everyone in the bright sun, as the wedding march blared from a record player. The minister appeared particularly uncomfortable, for he was heavily clothed and robed.

Just as the ceremony concluded, the owner's wife screamed from a shed beneath the house. They had stored the wedding cake there, because it was the coolest place. Alas, it was not cool enough. All three top tiers had slipped and oozed to the ground. Only the bottom layer was still edible. That, plus too much champagne, drunk by roasting, parched guests, made for a hilarious reception.

When the procession marched out of the local high school, it was not for a graduation. It was the end of a $30,000 wedding with 4,500 guests.

Although the groom was a minister, he could find no church with space enough for the four honor attendants, 14 junior brides-maids, 23 bridesmaids, three best men, 14 junior groomsmen, 24 groomsmen, two flower girls, two "tail bearers" (train bearers), one ring bearer and a miniature bride and groom, not to mention the minister and the wedding couple (95 in all – count them).

The bride, a gospel singer who had made good, explained that she came from multi-generational poverty and had resolved that, when she tied the knot, she would "do it up good."

In this marriage made in heaven, the Iowan bride and groom nodded their "I dos" en route from a plane to the ground in a skydiving free fall.

The bride wore a white nylon gown and a white veil on her helmet. The entire wedding party surrounded the airborne couple. No minister could be found to perform the in-air ceremony, so a friend was allowed to ask the important questions. His "thumbs up" signaled that they were man and wife.

In the state where bumper stickers read, "If God were not a Tar Heel, why is the sky Carolina blue?," a wedding held in Chapel Hill during a football game is a sacrilege. At least, so thought the bride's aunt, who had not missed a home game in years.

Actually, the time of the wedding should not have coincided with the kickoff, but the game time varied from the University of North Carolina's printed schedule to accommodate network television. And so, the aunt had to choose between the wedding and the game.

Or did she? Yes, she took her place in the pew, but she wore an earplug attached to her transistor radio, so as not to miss a single play.

On the next family wedding held during a Carolina game, she took a miniature TV set.

A Jeep dealership is an unusual enough place for a marriage ceremony – but a lion's cage at a Jeep dealership "takes the wedding cake."

In Michigan, a 49-year-old lion tamer married his assistant, witnessed by assorted felines and friends. The be-cameraed humans remained on the other side of the iron bars. The bride carried a bouquet; the groom, a whip.

The scene was a suburban restaurant, where the bride was a waitress and the groom had been a waiter. For both, it was a second marriage. Over 200 guests, many of whom were restaurant customers, had come. Most of the furniture was parked outside in a truck. In the two-minute ceremony, the couple spoke their own fabricated vows, and the pronouncement was made by a fellow who had been ordained by mail-order: the bartender.

Her neighbor was married in – of all places – a cemetery. Seems the bride had promised her grandmother, now deceased, that she would marry in one (not necessarily the grandmother's plot, any cemetery).

"Yes," said the neighbor, "they rode up in a hearse, and the pastor and some friends were there. The hearse waited for them, and they got back in and left." The young woman paused, anticipating a question, but answered before I could ask. "Some of our other neighbors wanted to know if I was invited. I told them, 'No, and I'm glad I wasn't, 'cause I wouldn't be caught dead there."

Examining Room No. 4 of the metropolitan hospital's emergency room was the site of a marriage ceremony in the late 1980s, The groom, who had been admitted at dawn of his wedding day, was lying in pain, awaiting surgery for appendicitis. Immediate family members and the matron-of-honor gathered to hear them speak their vows four hours sooner than expected. The only music was a squawking hospital intercom. Wedding chimes played at the end of the service: his new brother-in-law's watch beeping at the stroke of noon.

A white bikini substituted for a bridal gown, and she wore little flowers around her head rather than a veil. The wedding party was attired in swimsuits. Guests had on typical poolside garb. Only the minister, an elderly man, had worn a dark, dry suit.

The couple had met playing volleyball in a swimming pool, so that's where they wanted to be joined in matrimony - although they were divided by a volleyball net during most of the service.

CNN News was there to record their nuptial kiss: the bride lifted the net and gave her hubby a wet smack.

An auto parts store was chosen by a High Point, North Carolina, bride. She wanted her wedding there because that is where she met her groom. On a Sunday, they stood between the antifreeze and the hubcaps to say their vows.

Wedding Attire

People expect certain clothing to be worn at a wedding. When someone deviates – planned or unplanned – from the norm, tongues will wag and tales will be told.

How solemn and stiff her fiance looked at the other end of the long aisle. Never, during the saying of their vows did he loosen up. Throughout the reception, he stood stock still in the receiving line, polite but strained. She nudged him in the ribs. "It's almost over now, you can relax," she gently teased.

"No, I can't," he replied, still standing straight as a telephone pole. "I'll explain later."

At last, when they were alone, he told of dressing at their brand new apartment. His tux zipper broke! And not a safety pin anywhere. He and his best man had scrambled through the four rooms, searching for anything which might hold his fly together for two or three hours. All they could find was a single dry cleaner's clip. They fastened it as best they could and hurried to the church. The poor groom dared not make any quick or vigorous moves.

Her consternation began when the bride realized that she had not measured the aisle before purchasing her gown with a hoop skirt. Her escort had to march a pace ahead, with her tripping awkwardly behind. Once the tears started rolling, she couldn't control them, through the rector's charge, her groom's vows and her own.

So flustered was she that, on her exit, she grasped the roses of her arm bouquet, pointing the handle toward the congregation, gun-toting style.

At an English-speaking church in Tokyo, the family of the Japanese groom watched politely as their relative took an American girl in marriage. Most of them probably could not understand the words of the ceremony. Certainly, they could not understand the bride's culture.

In Japan, a bride traditionally wears a red and white kimono (red is the color of celebration) and an elaborate headdress upon lacquered hair. On her face, she wears heavy make-up. If the makeup cracks, that is a disgrace to the family, for the bride is expected to be demure, dignified and restrained. Both families play major roles in the whole affair.

This bride had no family in Japan. The minister's wife stood in for her mother. The young American woman had long straight hair and wore a glistening white wedding dress with a mini-skirt. Had she put on white makeup, it most definitely would have cracked.

At the reception, a formal dinner in a restaurant, the older males stood up and made speeches, according to custom. Had she been like other brides, she would have sat with her eyes cast down and her expression solemn. Instead, the effervescent girl jumped up and responded to their kind words like a cheerleader in a short uniform. Her husband was immensely pleased. But the old men were confused. And the groom's family were humiliated.

Happily for the couple, they did not remain in Japan. The Japanese in-laws never showed anyone their wedding pictures.

The uncle-of-the-bride's suspenders snapped apart at the center back, moments before he was to escort his niece down the aisle. His 200-pound frame was too much for the elderly elastic. In a flurry, a bridesmaid found a tiny brass safety pin, fastened the frayed straps and hurried away.

Waiting for the traditional wedding march to begin, the bride weakened. "Uncle Carter, I think I'm going to faint."

"We'll both faint, if this safety pin pops," he said.

For years, she was known as the laughing bride in that little Virginia town.

Tears were mussing the mother-of-the-groom's face. "Tell me a joke," she whispered to her husband, as they were settling into the first pew, "so I'll stop crying."

"Look at my lap," he whispered back.

Her tears stopped immediately, when she saw his open fly. His zipper had broken right before he was to enter the church. No one around him could find a safety pin. It was too late to do anything but follow his wife to their seats.

Later, in the receiving line at the reception, he still had the broken zipper, temporarily closed with a pin. But the story had spread, so he was explaining to a few of their friends how he had felt during the wedding: "With all the embarrassment, I didn't know whether I could stick it out."

Now he's more embarrassed over the statement than over the zipper.

The mother-of-the-bride was extremely nervous. She stopped in the ladies room one last time just before her turn to enter the sanctuary. Soon she was headed down the aisle, her long pink gown flowing as she walked with all eyes upon her. In her hand, she was clutching a roll of pink toilet paper. Her pink clutch purse was still in the ladies room.

She felt it pop – knew immediately that the button holding her hoop slip was gone. The Iowa bride could hardly concentrate on her vows for wondering what to do when she had to turn around.

As the first notes of the recessional were played, she made her decision. She spun around and stepped out of the hoop. Her wedding gown collapsed around her, and she left her slip at the altar

In the most staid "old line" church in Columbus, Georgia, there was an enormous wedding with ten or eleven groomsmen, an equal number of bridesmaids and all the pomp and circumstance expected.

But the groomsmen look grim, every one. That is, until the organ trumpeted the bride's entrance. Then they each broke into a huge grin, with every other tooth blackened.

Some in the congregation gasped. Others got tickled. The minister, whose back was to the piano-key smiles, looked puzzled, but began the opening statements. Further into the ceremony, the groom's shoulders shook, as he tried to stifle a laugh. Chuckles within the congregation crescendoed into loud laughter, and still, only the stodgy minister was oblivious to the joke.

It was just as well. He wouldn't have thought it was funny.

The groomsman had rushed into town right before the rehearsal and had been too otherwise occupied (and pickled and pie-eyed) to try on the rented morning coat before the ceremony. Jerking it on over his white shirt just before his ushering job began, he felt it split from collar to tail. Too late to mend it, he wore it anyway with the white "skunk stripe" down his back.

Her friend had advised, "You know all the groom's mother should do is wear beige and keep your mouth shut."

But on her son's wedding day, the loquacious lady wore neon blue with shimmering spangles. She was receiving guests on the lawn of her elegant home, where the wedding was held. A rabbi had just performed the traditional Hebrew ceremony, although neither the bride nor the groom (only the groom's mother) were Jewish.

Her friend, eyeing the bespangled dress remarked, "I see you didn't wear beige, and I'll bet you didn't keep your mouth shut."

She frowned. "No, and that's why everybody's mad at me."

These dresses did double-duty: when two sisters got married a few hours apart, they had the same attendants wearing the same dresses. A bridal shop seamstress worked at the church between ceremonies to altar the first bride's gown to fit the second and to change the size of the bridesmaid's dress, so that the first bride could stand up for her sister.

The groom's father wore patched glasses over his black eye. He and the groom were both decorated with colorful bruises. En route to the rehearsal, another driver, who didn't care for the way the father was driving, had run them off the road and attacked them with a baseball bat.

At a tuxedo rental shop, the manager tried to tell the bride's mother that she could not change all the outfits. Only the bride or groom could do that, the clerk declared. The mother insisted. Later, the groom called to re-instate the original order. Apparently, the bride's mother upset a few other people. At the reception, some of her new in-laws threw her into the pool.

All the bridesmaids and ushers wore bluejeans. The bride had a matching denim skirt. An outdoor wedding in a pastoral setting? No indeed. This one was in a Kentucky church. The reception was a covered dish dinner, featuring creamed corn and fried okra.

"I don't need to." Remember when your two-year-old used to protest with those words, as she was being led to the potty? Well, brides invariably say that to their bridal consultants before the gown goes on. And many a bride has wrinkled a dress or stained a slip while smushed into a bathroom stall.

Many people have tales of attire problems:

• The wedding gown, pressed at the last minute, which had an iron-sized hole in the rump. The bride's mother folded, layered and pinned it, instructing her daughter not to sit down during or after the ceremony.

• The dress with no wearer. A bridesmaid broke her leg right before the wedding and had to be replaced. No one among the bride's family could fit into the dress. But a cousin of the groom, who wore that size, was found just in time.

• The lost gown. While the bride frantically waited in her underwear in the bride's room, friends were calling around to find out what happened. The store representative insisted that it had been dropped off at the church earlier that day. Just "in the nick of time," the senior pastor of a nearby church sprinted in, dress in hand, to make the delivery.

• The bridesmaid's dress that was not hemmed by the store and had to be pinned minutes before she went down the aisle. Each step caused a scratch.

Others tell of unusual wedding attire:

• The black lace wedding gown, beaded and bejeweled, for an all-black-attire wedding. The bride had it fashioned in the South, but took it to New York for the ceremony. Smart gal.

• Dirty tennis shoes worn with his tuxedo by one of the wealthiest bachelors-turned-groom in town.

• Lanterns strung together with beflowered ribbons carried by all the bridesmaids. Problems: timing and spacing, as they bungled and bumped their way down and back up the aisle.

• Overalls worn by the groom's father. Although he was from a rural area and it was his usual daytime garb, the rest of the males had on suits for the big-city wedding.

• The groom's slightly worn shoes with soles painted black especially for the occasion. The bride had them painted to look new when the couple kneeled.

• A handmade fly in place of the boutonniere of an avid trout fisherman, the groom.

• Clown makeup and gloves on the groom. His buddies, in revenge for his mean pranks, had painted him with India ink.

Disruptions

The more formal the ceremony and the more members of the wedding party, the more likely there will be a disruption.

People who attended weddings several decades ago recall the kerplunks of the ones who passed out from lack of air-conditioning. Others couldn't blame the heat.

In the 1930s, a groom fainted repeatedly during a church service. When revived the third time, he ran out - never to return. Friends said he was too much of a gentleman to admit he didn't want to marry the girl who had suddenly become infatuated with him.

Not only was it a "scorcher" summer day in the West Texas crossroads town, but the church's air-conditioning system had burned out. For that reason, the service had been planned for the evening. Even so, the sanctuary was stifling hot.

All the males in the wedding party, however, wore their entire formal regalia. Almost as soon as they arrived in front, the minister allowed them to be seated on the first row to avoid fainting. Only the groom, best man and clergyman stood among the women. The bride helped to steady her husband-to-be, as he reeled from the heat.

Just after the couple had followed the minister up into the chancel for their vows, the best man, en route up the few chancel steps, fell with a crash. His body hit a guitar which had been leaning against the organ. He conked his head on the floor and sprawled, stone still.

The mother-of-the-groom, who was also the best man's mother, became hysterical. Her own husband had passed away at 47. Other males in that family had died of heart attacks in their 40s. She was certain her son was dead or dying, too.

Fortunately, there was a doctor among the guests. He rushed up to attend the best man, who was unconscious. The physician quickly determined that he had merely passed out from the heat. Not quite so easily, he managed to convince the distraught mother that her son was not going to die. Meanwhile, everyone sat quietly watching the drama. When the service resumed and the wedding party recessed, the best man remained motionless on the floor.

On a sultry summer afternoon in the mid-'50s, a wedding party was assembled in a Presbyterian church with no air-conditioning in Washington, D.C.

The minister was asking the questions, when the groom began to tilt. Leaning a bit to that side, the clergyman continued. As the groom tilted more, he bent even further, still reading, down almost to the floor. The young man collapsed in a faint. His groomsman rushed to revive him and stand him back up.

"Are you certain you want to go on?" asked the minister.

"Yes, yes," he replied weakly. Surely, he must have seen his fiancee's tears. As the next words were being read, the poor fellow seemed to melt like a candle, right onto the floor, dropping slowly but straight down. While the bride withdrew to a corner crying, he was being stretched out on a pew. Finally, someone propped him up on the seat.

By then, the organist had stopped playing and was leaning over the railing above the pulpit, peering at the spectacle.

Meanwhile, the church secretary, a guest, recalled that a member who was a doctor was doing a volunteer job in a nearby church building. Soon, the physician, clad in painting clothes, was striding down the center aisle, and the secretary was tripping along the left aisle, pointing and explaining, "He's a doctor. He's a doctor. A doctor."

A quick examination and a sniff of ammonia later, the groom was looking better. The physician fetched the church wheelchair.

Unsure whether the bridegroom was more than just physically faint-hearted, the clergyman questioned if he still wanted to get married. He nodded that he did, to the rhythm of his bride's "boo-hoos."

The last the minister ever saw of that couple was the two of them retreating up the aisle, the bride in her flowing white gown, pushing her new husband in a wheelchair.

That summer day in the late 1960s was exceedingly hot, and a flu epidemic was rampant. The service in the unair-conditioned Lutheran church was lengthy but not at all curtailed when an acolyte flipped over the rail, having fainted from the heat and the illness. One usher collapsed on the floor; then another. No one moved them. Of the "show must go on" school, the minister merely stepped over the one in the way to complete his part. He and the rest of the wedding party marched out, leaving the three prone in the chancel.

In the early '70s, a Georgia bridegroom fainted, and only his best man and the bride knew it. Anticipating the possibility, the best man had positioned himself behind his friend to hold him up. He even answered the vows on the groom's behalf. When the groom awoke, he was nearly married.

When a rector asked the groom, "Wilt thou...?" he did. He wilted right down to the floor.

"Preacher, I think I'm going to faint," whispered the knit-browed bride, while the soloist was singing two-thirds of the way through a formal service.

"No, you're not," he replied in a low voice. "Just bend your knees and take some deep breaths."

She obeyed but grew whiter. "Preacher, I'm going to throw up," she said.

"Faint!" he barked.

Why do brides want young children in their weddings? To take the limelight off themselves? To give comic relief to the tension? Certainly, they add uncertainty. Here are just a few examples:

His diminutive white tuxedo was immaculate. The rings were attached to the fancy white pillow. The two-and-a-half-year-old marched big-boy style to the front of the church, joining the others as rehearsed. For a few moments, he even held the hand of a bridesmaid as planned.

But that was boring. It was much more fun to throw the pillow as high as possible and catch it over and over. Then he slid the stuffed white satin square up and down the front pew, until his mother interrupted his play and pulled him out of view.

To the dismay of the Chattanooga pastor, the bride insisted on having not one but two preschool children in the wedding. Furthermore, they would go into the upper chancel where the rings were to be exchanged.

His fears were allayed when the rehearsal went well. But during the actual ceremony, the children got into a noisy tussle. All the while they were in the upper chancel, the kids were having a tug-of-war. The flower girl jealously demanded to hold the pillow, and the ring bearer was guarding it with his life. No parent stepped up or spoke up. The pastor raised his voice and raced through the rest of the service.

Ann's role was to sprinkle rose petals from her basket ahead of the bride. One by one, she did just that. But nearly halfway to her destination, the three-year-old grew tired. Yawning, she sat down to rest on the floor.

"Ann, come on!" stage-whispered her mother, the matron-of-honor.

Perhaps Ann heard. Or perhaps she decided on her own to perform. She stood up and dumped all the rest of the petals mid-aisle before hurrying on her way.

Another tyke with a basketful of petals distributed some of her floral bits along her way to the semi-circle of attendants. But while the bride and groom were solemnly making their vows of love and fidelity and the guests were at the peak of emotional empathy, she realized that she had a large surplus of undistributed petals. Whereupon, she upended the basket and vigorously jumped up and down on the residue. She plunged the whole assembly into irrepressible laughter, puncturing the mood of solemnity and breaking up the ceremony.

In a Methodist church with a communion rail at the front of the sanctuary, a small flower girl got bored mid-ceremony. Climbing upon the rail, she turned toward the congregation and made faces at them.

The children followed their rehearsal instructions quite well, until the ring bearer, age 4, signaled his mother that he had to go to the bathroom. While she took him to relieve himself, two of the flower girls fought over who would hold the ring bearer's pillow. They tugged and tossed, but the bride and groom were oblivious to it all. Only when the ring bearer retrieved "his" property did the fight end.

Two three-year-olds were the center of attention in a Virginia church wedding. The flower girl, with her basket of unscattered rose petals, made it to the front. But as soon as the bride got in place, she raced to her father, the photographer. He took her and his camera out, never to return.

Meanwhile, the ring bearer was facing the congregation and picking his nose. Then he spied his six-year-old girl cousin at whom he poked out his tongue. Still with his back turned to the bride and groom, he put the lacy ring cushion on his head and peeked between the streamers. Seeing his mother's crooking finger, he left the chancel and joined her on the second row. The rings were fakes, so his presence was not essential.

A little more than a toddler, the ring bearer had taken his place among the wedding party in front of the church. The vows were being spoken when the little fellow mumbled something to an usher and promptly stained the carpet at his feet.

All three children, ages two to five, behaved beautifully at the wedding of their favorite baby-sitter. They watched intently, as she went down to the front with her father, said a few words and returned with her husband. "Mommy, Mommy!" shouted the three-year-old. "She's leaving with another man!"

Of course, children aren't the only ones who cause disruptions:

In the late 1960s, a scorned suitor phoned the bride-to-be with a threat. "You will not marry that guy," he said. "I'll find a way to stop the wedding."

Though rattled, the young woman was determined to marry the man she loved when and where she had planned. She informed the preacher of the problem and instructed him to go on, no matter what.

Sure enough, the jilted lover, who had a pilot's license, found a way to disrupt the ceremony: nose dives – zooming, booming ones – above the church. He began before the service started and kept buzzing the church over and over.

"That fool wouldn't crash the plane into the church!" thought the preacher, praying that his own statement was true. He went on, trying to ignore the ferocious racket.

After about the tenth dive, the vengeful pilot was waved away by another airman, who ordered him via radio to leave. The bride's father had anticipated such an antic and notified the local airport to send someone up to stop it.

As the pilot flew out of his ex-sweetheart's life, the preacher pronounced her married to his rival.

In a run-down section of Trenton, New Jersey, a bride and groom were surrounded by relatives and friends from the South and West, who had come to see them repeat their vows in an old Catholic Church.

The Southerners and a few Westerners, mostly Protestants, were unnerved by the lack of privacy during the ceremony. Odd people, unconnected with the wedding party, were milling around. Right before time for the groom and best man to step out, a filthy urchin ran noisily down the aisle and through a door to the right. Moments later, the dirty face appeared above an acolyte's robe and grimy fingers performed the assigned tasks. An elderly woman, who had been seated in the rear, fumbled to open a window, while attendants were making their entrance.

Just as the petite flower girl began dropping petals, an irreverent photographer jumped in front of her and backed down the aisle, snapping shots. He stopped the bewildered pink-clad child to get a better pose.

When it was the bride's turn, he repeated his rudeness. Throughout the opening of the ceremony, he snapped away, flashing bulbs and edging around the wedding party to get different angles. The priest shook his head but was ignored.

At the point in the service when the bride presents her bouquet to the Virgin Mary, the photographer bounced behind her. Reverently, she placed the floral gift on an altar and started back down the three or four steps.

"Wait!" the photographer ordered. "Go back. I haven't got my shot."

"That will be enough," commanded the priest, in an equally loud voice. The photographer snapped again.

"SIT DOWN!" the priest shouted. He refused to continue until the disrupter was seated.

When the preacher asked whether anyone present knew of any reason why the couple should not be joined together in holy matrimony, the bride turned and said, "I do."

She glanced at one of her attendants and back at her guests. "I would like to thank my maid-of-honor for sleeping with my fiance." With that, she whapped the groom in the face with her bouquet of roses and walked out.

Why didn't she just cancel the ceremony? Friends said that the wedding was all paid for, so she got to show off her dress and show down the ones who had done her wrong.

Throughout the preparations for a wedding in a Chicago apartment, the minister was annoyed by the "yapping, yapping, yapping" of the family dog.

"I thought the lady of the house, or the man, would put the dog out," recalled the preacher. "But no one did." The fuzzy yapper took his place among the attendants and barked along with the vows.

No tears for this nervous bride. She giggled through the charge. She giggled during the music. She giggled over the vows and while her brand new husband placed the ring on her finger. Not soft chuckles, but high-pitched giggles which resounded throughout the church.

Imagine the embarrassment of the bride when she threw up in the middle of the ceremony. Her minister made the best of the situation by stretching her out on the front pew and reminding her guests that everyone has difficult moments in their lives. He called for a recess until they could clean her up and get her back on her feet.

"Mama, guess how many hymns they're going to sing at the wedding!" said an exasperated bridesmaid in a phone call after the rehearsal. Before her mother could reply, she told her. "Seven. One of them is America the Beautiful, and all of a sudden, some woman in a uniform hops up out of the congregation, rushes to the front and salutes a flag."

A disruption? Apparently, the bride didn't think so. But the bridesmaid did.

Mishaps and Misquotes

An average Protestant or civil ceremony lasts fifteen to twenty minutes. In such a short time, what could go wrong? Plenty!

Although they were supposed to have been dripless candles, the florist had placed plastic on the floor beneath the candelabra. The air-conditioning blew a bit of a gale, though, causing those dripless tapers to drip during the church ceremony.

As the bride and groom, maid-of-honor and best man were departing, the heat of the wax puddles ignited the plastic. Only the bride's father, who was still seated in the pew, noticed. All he could do was look wide-eyed, point and say, "Ah...oh...ah." His guttural sounds caught the attention of the preacher.

Abruptly, the clergyman turned to stamp it out. The organist played louder and harder. The soloist screamed a soprano "Oh my God!" But the fire burned on.

The preacher stamped and stomped, as flames bounced between his legs up inside his robe. He jerked that up in "tiptoe through the tulips" fashion and kept stamping all the more to the frantic organist's tune until the fire was extinguished.

Later, the organist explained that he thought it was the organ in flames, and he was determined to play it until it died.

An operatic-trained musician was to sing at his best friend's wedding. The bride's mother, however, requested that he sing *I Love You Truly*. He detested the song, but learned it and dutifully ran through it at the rehearsal.

But when he opened his mouth to sing it at the ceremony, his mind went blank. To the tune played by the organist he sang, "I love you truly. Truly dear. Truly I love you. Truly dear. Looove you truly, so truuuuly...."

Second verse: "Truly I love you. So truly dear...."

Third verse: "So truly I love you..."

Afterward, the mother-of-the-bride raved about how beautifully he sang the song. She never noticed his improvised wording.

Two preachers, one young and one retired, were officiating at a night wedding in a large rural church. The younger one finished his part and passed the book over to his colleague.

As the retired preacher was adjusting his book so he could read it with his older eyes, he got it too close to the candelabra. The corner of the book caught fire! He fumbled to put it out. No luck.

The quick-moving groom, however, snuffed it out with his hand, leaving the groom with a smoked palm and the bride with a scorched wedding book.

The minister sensed something was amiss when he and his brother, the groom, were preparing to enter the chancel. Tears were streaming down his sibling's face.

All through the opening of the service more tears quietly fell. When he reached the "Will you..." part, the groom opened his mouth wide. "Wahhhhh!" he bawled loudly like a baby.

As a brother, the minister's first inclination was to grab him by the shoulders and shake him. Instead, he maintained the compassionate pastor role and calmed the embarrassed bridegroom.

A change in heart? Shocking news about his intended? Nope. Just the emotion of the moment.

Spike heels had just come into vogue, but the building and grounds committee of the historical church had not brought the sanctuary in "sync" with the times yet.

Thus, when a bridesmaid came through the threshold en route

to the altar and wobbled a bit to the right, her heel caught in a wooden heating grate. The organ kept playing, but she didn't move.

Daintily, the flustered attendant attempted to remove her shoe from the grate without stooping. No luck. She jerked her knee upward. Her foot came up, but not the shoe. The music played on, and the congregation was turning to see what the holdup was.

Once more, the pretty woman tried the jerking action with her shoe back on. Up came the tinted satin shoe, grate and all! And down the aisle she went, clunking every other step.

The bride's family had *Philadelphia Story* prestige. VIPs from up and down the East Coast and farther assembled for this Pennsylvania wedding in the 1960s.

An usher still remembers the awe he felt as he helped unfurl the runner down the aisle amid all that wealth and power. Just as he passed the pew where the Pughs of Standard Oil were seated, the edge of the runner snagged on a heat register. The rest of the folded aisle cloth popped out of his hand, bopping Mrs. Pugh in the head, knocking off her hat.

That incident settled the usher's future plans; he would never settle in that part of the country.

It was a Catholic wedding, but a Presbyterian minister was allowed to assist two priests. One of the priests instructed his Protestant counterpart from the side of his mouth: "Read the scripture." The Presbyterian carefully obeyed each gentle command.

When the vows had been pronounced, "congratulate the bride and groom" spurred him to step forward toward the couple. But he reacted too fast to "kiss the bride." He beat the groom to her lips.

At the rehearsal, the groom had asked when he could kiss the bride. "After the final amen," he had been told.

When he heard the "amen" at the ceremony, he kissed her lovingly. But she, and others throughout the church, laughed.

Wrong cue: that had been the "amen" after the invocation.

Her old-fashioned wedding gown had lace sleeves, pointed and looped over her middle fingers. In her right hand, the bride carried a lace handkerchief.

When it was time to light the unity candle, she and her mate each reached for individual candles, which they would use to unite two flames into one on the larger candle's wick.

The bride's white candle was stuck tight in its holder. She twisted and pulled. Her right hand slid upward, and the flame whooshed into her handkerchief and onto the lace sleeve.

Shaking and squealing, she – with plenty of help – snuffed it out before she got seriously burned.

Then there was the one about the bride who couldn't move. Well, she made it down the aisle but couldn't seem to get back.

When the prayer was concluded, the groom rose up from his knees, but the bride didn't. He pulled on her arm. She seemed frozen. He pulled harder. She toppled to one side. He pulled again. She crumpled on the floor. Picking her up, he carried her to a nearby bench. His beloved was out cold.

A bit of fanning and shaking later, the bride was moved to an ante-room, and the pastor announced a fifteen-minute delay. Chairs were brought, and the ceremony continued with the couple seated.

On the second try, the bride did fine. Then it was time to leave. Standing, they turned around and took a few steps. But the groom went a pace or two ahead. The bride stood stock still. He pulled. She did not move. He pulled again. The third tug was a yank, and the loud rrrrripping of her train explained her immobility.

Misquotes are almost as common as mishaps during a ceremony. For most of the "actors" in the performance, it is their only time to play their parts in the spotlight. And yet, it is often the more experienced preacher who goofs.

He was called to "pinch hit" for a friend, this out-of-town minister, so he did not know the couple he would be marrying. Their sordid reputation had preceded them, though. Succinctly put, the man had left his first wife for the new bride, a divorcee also.

Halfheartedly, the minister went through the routine by rote until he got to the part in the charge where he intended to say, "Our Savior has declared that a man shall leave his father and mother and cleave unto his wife."

Inadvertently, he said, "That a man shall leave his wife and cleave.." He skimmed over the rest, hoping no one noticed his slip of the tongue.

The brand new preacher memorized the wording for his first wedding ceremony, just as his seminary professor had suggested. "What should I do if I forget?" he had asked that professor.

"Just say whatever scripture comes to mind," his mentor said.

Well, he did forget. And the verse that tumbled out was, "Lord, forgive them, for they know not what they do."

In his opening remarks, a pastor quoted – or rather, misquoted – from Genesis 2:18. "It is good," he said, "that man should live alone."

No one there, especially the bride, will ever let him forget it.

During the exchanging of rings, the couple, both members of his church, recited after him, "With these wings I thee wed."

Now, whenever they see their minister, they "flap" hello.

When the pastor read the part which goes, "If anyone knows any cause why this marriage should not take place, let him speak now or forever hold his peace," the groom responded, "I do."

Hoping the fellow had nervously "jumped the gun," the clergyman ignored the reply.

47

Ring, Ring...

That circle of unbroken love, which is a part of almost every wedding, can be another source of consternation when tensions are great. Sometimes, it's "ring, ring, where's the ring?" Sometimes, there's another problem.

Our daughter, Joy, was two years old when the Director of Christian Education at our church was married. Every detail was planned with children in mind, even the low table at the reception with cake and candy for the toddlers. The bride emphasized to parents that she expected all ages to come. She may have regretted that, though, during the exchanging of rings.

I described in a whisper to our little girl what was happening. Suddenly, she angrily pointed her finger at the groom. In her loudest two-year-old voice, she shouted, "Tommy give Joy ring, too!"

En route to the church, the best man was wearing the bride's ring on his little finger. When he shifted gears, the ring dropped off and, in some strange way, with a clink and a clunk, deposited itself into the defroster slot and down into the car's heater.

He pulled in front of the church, reached under the dashboard and tried to figure out how to extract the ring. He fumbled and grumbled but saw no way to retrieve the band that had been entrusted to him.

Inside the church, he solicited help from the pastor, who could only send him to the nearest service station.

At the station, the attendant, in his haste, tore the heater all to pieces. But he found the ring – mangled.

The bride had the ring all right. But apparently she had purchased the wrong size. When it would not slide onto her groom's finger, she tried pushing it with all her strength.

The groom grimaced. When that didn't work, she tried screwing it on with both hands. For at least two minutes, she pushed and turned the ring. It never *did* get on his hand.

At the rehearsal, someone demonstrated to the preacher how to pull the end of the tiny ribbon bow, so that he could slip the bands off the ring bearer's pillow.

But before the actual event, the ring-tie-on-person had made a bow atop a square knot. A gentle tug on the end did not loosen the ribbons; it pulled them tighter.

Hard as he tried, the preacher could not release those rings. He tugged. He pulled. He picked at it.

On the third row, a woman noticed his dilemma. She walked up to the front, pulled a pair of scissors out of her pocketbook and cut the ribbon.

Fortunately for the errant matron-of-honor who had left the groom's ring in a dressing room, the pastor was her father. "Gimme your college ring," she whispered out of the side of her mouth, just after they had stepped up into the chancel.

"What?" he whispered back. He complied when he understood.

The bride balked at accepting the wrong ring from her sister, but gave it over to be blessed, when she saw that she had no choice.

Someone wondered later, "Did that mean that her husband married her father?"

This Alabama church, built at the turn of the century, had a flat seating area and a raised chancel.

As the groom's ring was being passed, someone bumbled and fumbled, and it dropped.

The floor was slanted, and it rolled – bling, bling, bling – with

50

two ushers, the groom and a man from the audience chasing it. Bling, bling – it hit a cold air return. Brrat-a-tat, brrat, brrat, brrat-a-tat. All four men were on all fours, watching the grate, listening – brrat, brrat, brrat-a-tat – as the ring dropped all the way to the furnace.

A short time before the wedding, the bride stopped by the church to check on arrangements. Somehow, the top of a piano fell on her finger – not a "pointer," not a thumb, but the one out of ten that she needed that day.

She was rushed to the hospital emergency room, where a huge bandage was applied. She made back to the church just in time, but had to present her left "pinky" to accept the ring.

One little ring bearer in a white suit used his fancy pillow for what pillows were intended to be used for. He dropped it to the floor and put his head on it.

Well, it *was* an hour-long service, and the two-year-old was tired.

A groom's mother tells of storing the wedding ring for safe-keeping and of retrieving it for her son the night before it was to be used. Fingering it, he handed it back, and she put it on a hall table. The next day, no one could find it. All day, they searched.

A bridesmaid, who worked for a jeweler in another town, called a local wholesaler. Perhaps he would have a duplicate ring for the bride's matched set. No, but he would loan a gorgeous diamond and ruby band to the distressed strangers for "appearances sake" on their honeymoon. Needless to say, the grateful bride worried about losing the precious loan but wore it with pride.

Eleven years later, the mother-of-the-groom reports that, despite a thorough search, the original band was never found.

Who's Who?

*Roles are pretty well set in traditional ceremonies. Only the
names are different – most of the time.*

Now in his 80s, a white-haired gentleman named Carter recalls
a wedding for which he was a "facilitator."

Carter and his two friends, Hugh and Lester, were real estate
salesmen during the Florida boom in 1925. Hugh's fiancee, Elizabeth,
came all the way from Virginia to find out whether she really loved
Hugh enough to marry him.

One night after dinner, Hugh borrowed Lester's car to take
Elizabeth out on a date. When neither car nor couple had returned
by 1:00 a.m., Lester and Carter began to worry. Hugh soon arrived
with the explanation that they had driven to Clearwater, the Pinellas
county seat, to get a marriage license. Hugh thought he could get the
county's clerk of court to come to the courthouse at night to issue
them a license. He was wrong.

The next day, the foursome hatched a plan to hold the wedding
that very night, despite the fact that Elizabeth had to work all day
and Hugh had an afternoon appointment to show some acreage a
considerable distance away. Lester and Carter would get the license,
call the Episcopal rector, and engage the parish house for 7:30 p.m.

The two drove to Clearwater, but the clerk of court told them
they must have a notarized form, signed by the bride, stating that she
was over 21. Carter and Lester stopped by a friend's loan office to
ask if the friend's notary would sign the form as though Elizabeth
were there. No way would that so-called friend break the law. And
no way would the Pinellas clerk of court believe it anyway.

So the pair headed for Hillsborough County. In a Tampa park,
they found just what they were looking for, a streetwalker. About 40

years of age and "ugly as a mud fence," she, indeed, "looked her occupation," remembered Carter.

Even so, Carter, the young bachelor, held up a five-dollar bill and told her how she would fit into their latest plan.

"Mister, I'd do anything for five dollars," said the whore.

"Anything" in this case meant being coached on her new name, address and desire to marry Hugh before going to another notary public's office to fill out the form. "Hugh" would be whichever of the schemers lost the toss of a coin. That was Lester.

"Boy, was I relieved. I didn't want even a stranger to think I would marry such a hag," recalled Carter with a chuckle.

As for the streetwalker, an actress she was not. Despite the rehearsals on the park bench, her staccato "My name... is...Elizabeth...and I...want to...marry Hugh" sounded like a first-grader trying to read a script. Even so, the notary, though dubious, signed and sealed the document so that the men could buy a license from the Hillsborough clerk of court.

By mid-afternoon, Lester and Carter were back in St. Pete, making the other arrangements.

At 7:00 p.m., they picked up the bride. Elizabeth was agitated because she had neither seen nor heard from Hugh. One minute before 7:30 p.m., Hugh rushed into the parish house, tying his tie.

They each proceeded with their parts. Lester was the best man. A man who had known Elizabeth only a few days, gave the bride away. Carter was no longer the "facilitator;" he was the bridesmaid.

"Simplest wedding I've ever been to," snickered Elizabeth at the conclusion. "I didn't have to do a thing. Maybe I'll do it again sometime."

The rector was startled. Lester looked guilty, and Carter feared the wedding would be declared invalid. It wasn't – until 30 years later, when the couple divorced.

The big-shot politician's daughter's summer wedding was destined to be the most stupendous ever witnessed by an almost-rural Georgia town in the 1930s. A graduate of Agnes Scott, the bride had hired a professional wedding director from Atlanta. Most all the "trimmings" were being trucked in from the state capital.

At the rehearsal, the male director barked orders to everyone, especially the youthful minister, who was somewhat intimidated. It was his first church wedding. Finally, the father-of-the-bride, a former football captain, exerted his own forceful nature against the haughty wedding director and told him off.

The church was lavishly decorated, when the wedding party arrived 45 minutes ahead of time. Every pew in the 200-seat sanctuary was already filled, and the caravan from Atlanta had not yet arrived!

The young minister nearly fainted from the heat and the panic, but the father took charge. He strode down to the front and politely asked everyone who was not invited to please go to the reception. It was being held at his palatial colonial home. "There's plenty of room on the lawn for everyone," he assured.

Eighty percent of the audience, most dressed in street clothes, filed out, right before the formally dressed Atlantans streamed in. But the townspeople were not ready to go to the reception. "Outsiders" were not the only ones who would see the show. They took whatever they could find to stand on, so that they could peer in the open windows on both sides of the sanctuary.

The minister, now retired, reports the end of the tale: that politician was never elected again.

From the expression on his face, the minister's wife knew he was in trouble. He was almost to the part where he would call the name of the bride to ask whether she would take the man at her side in marriage.

Her husband had performed the ceremony for the groom and his first wife, too, and all four of them had been friends. She knew that, as their pastor, it must be difficult for him to look Bride No. 2 in the eye. In fact, his eyes, just then, were darting with uncertainty; but they never noticed her lips, as she mouthed the name of the second wife: "Madeline."

He paused. Undoubtedly, he had forgotten to write the names in the little wedding book he held in his hands.

The wife of the minister tried again. "Mad-e-line." But he wasn't looking in her direction.

"Let us pray," he said.

She smiled, hoping no one else would notice the unplanned prayer. Peeking, she watched him, as he spoke extemporaneously and simultaneously sidled over to a small table in the chancel where the marriage certificate lay.

He moved back into place. "Amen. Madeline, will you take..."

"Ron, will you have Kay to be your wife..." read the preacher from the wedding book. "Kay, will you have Ron?"

The groom calmly said his part: "I, Ben, take you Kay..."

Immediately, the preacher realized his mistake. He had written in the name of a new summer intern instead of the groom. Kay had pledged herself to Ron, to live with him and cherish him!

When it was again her turn, he made sure he said, "I, Kay take you, Ben," and stuck in the pledge that she had made to Ron, which, surely, would supersede her first one.

Ever hear of a ten-year-old maid-of-honor?

I was one for my cousin/sister. My first cousin's parents had died when she was young, so she had lived with us since I was a year old.

"You're the only sister I'll ever have," she explained, as I beamed with adoration and pride.

Because I was tall for my age, I was certain no one would realize how young I was. I felt truly grown up, until I lifted my long taffeta skirt to ascend a couple of steps in the chancel.

"Awwwww," I heard a chatterbox woman say in more than a whisper. "Look at those cute little white socks."

I melted back to my ten-year-old status.

As the bride and her father reached the chancel, they did not stop according to tradition. Together, they went around the communion table to face their guests. The rector, wedding party and guests stared wide-eyed.

The bride spoke, "Thank you for coming, but there will be no wedding today. The reception is set up downstairs, and you are all invited to enjoy yourselves there."

She and her father continued around the communion table, stopping next to the maid-of-honor. She turned to the girl and croaked indignantly, "You bitch! You had him last night. You can have him forever!"

Episcopal weddings, as a rule, are quite proper. Especially in this back-straightening, liturgical, upper-crust church.

Everything went exactly as it should have. Every participant was as dignified as the church itself.

Except the groom. At the back of the church, he, Tarzan, grabbed his Jane, threw her over his shoulder, and ran out.

This Nevada wedding was so remote that, to get there, the minister and his wife had to cut through the nuclear testing grounds. Actually, guards did the cutting, and repairing, of a barbed wire fence to let them through.

Once at the site of the wilderness wedding, they saw the bride still picking wildflowers for her bouquet. No matter. The minister could be as laid back as the participants, and he waited calmly.

But even this Las-Vegas-conditioned clergyman was taken aback when the best man, with a bandana around his neck, was introduced. The best man was a dog.

The ushers seated the 200 guests. The candles were lit at the front of the United Methodist Church. The organ was playing. The bridesmaids were assembled, and the bride looked lovely in her wedding gown. But the minister stood alone at the front.

He welcomed the friends and families of the couple who had been married a few hours earlier in the local hospital emergency room, just before the groom underwent an appendectomy. He invited everyone to join the bride at the reception.

Almost everything went on as had been planned month ahead. The organist played all the pieces except the processional. There was a receiving line. Their photographer even took pictures, minus the groom. The soloist left out only one song: *Entreat Me Not to Leave Thee.*

A double wedding is unusual. An octonary ("octople?") one is downright odd, particularly when the marriage proposal has been made by a public body.

In Chicago, in the late '80s, the group wedding for eight couples was arranged by the Chicago Housing Authority to help keep former heads-of-household, all female, from getting evicted. Their boyfriends were illegal residents, thus causing the women to have a lease violation and be subject to eviction.

When the Housing Authority enforced the lease to combat gang violence, residents were angry at first. But their violence subsided, and at least eight couples seemed pleased by the Authority's "marriage proposal."

The brides all wore pink gowns, offered by a local dressmaker; the grooms, free rental tuxedos.

It was aggravating enough that her veil kept falling off before and during the home ceremony and that her brother kept rewinding the tape of wedding music, screeching it excessively. But the bride was most unnerved when the minister repeatedly called her by her mother's name in the vows.

"Who gives this woman to be married to this man?" the preacher asked. The nervous father-of-the-bride answered, "Her father and I do."

The minister asked, "Who gives this man to marry this woman?"

The bride's startled father quickly responded, "His mother and I do."

At his first wedding after his ordination, this minister did admirably until he pronounced the bride and groom "man and husband."

The bride was quite a fine soloist and elected to sing at her own wedding. After their vows had been made, she turned and gazed into her beloved's eyes while she sang, "I'd rather have Jesus..."

That the ceremony was held in a nightclub was extraordinary enough. That most of the wedding party and 150 guests wore black added a macabre touch to what the groom, lead singer in a destructo-rock band, called an "anti-wedding."

But what truly surprised observers at this late-1980s wedding was the choice of attendants: a woman was the best man; a man was the flower girl. The flower girl pulled a puckish preschool prank – he poured rose petals into the lap of a family member.

Money, Money

Some people say that the father-of-the-bride's main function is to write checks. But other people connected with a wedding think of money, too.

"Magistrates are not allowed to travel, so they called me," said the chaplain of a predominantly female college. "They didn't want to be married in the magistrate's office or the chapel at the jail."

She agreed to marry the strangers, if they would come for counseling. Three times, the couple, who were in their fifties, came. This, she discovered, would be his third marriage, her second. The ceremony was to be held at a lake nearly 30 miles from town.

"At the lake" really meant "on the lake," and they wanted her to "come down to see the boat" the evening before. Out a stretch of highway, down a dirt road, another dirt road and another she drove until a goat obstructed her path. She shooed him off and arrived promptly at the spot where she was to meet them. Neither was in sight, so she ho-hummed in the car for a half an hour before knocking on the door of a nearby cabin. A somewhat scantily dressed man appeared. Yes, they were going to use his boat for the wedding, but he did not know the couple very well. He called his wife, who was reasonably cordial but could not seem to get it through her head who this chaplain was.

When she asked for the third time: "You're the minister's wife?" the tall young chaplain replied, "No, I'm the minister, and if you ask me again, I'm going to get angry."

At last, the awaited pair arrived, with neither an excuse nor an apology. They went on with showing her the pontoon boat and explaining how it would round the nearby spit of land and make a floating processional into the cove where their friends would be waiting. Some of them would wade out to hold the boat like human anchors during the ceremony.

61

As the chaplain was leaving, the bride called out after her, "Wear blue! Everyone is wearing blue."

That Southern August day was hot and so was the chaplain's only blue dress, but she wore it anyway. She regretted it the moment she arrived, for all the wedding guests were in t-shirts, shorts and swimsuits. By 2:00 p.m., the time of the wedding, the bride and groom were nowhere in sight. Someone at the cabin suggested she "go over to the trailer." She obeyed, and waited nearly an hour with some guys who were drinking. When they decided to get dressed for the wedding, she decided to take a walk.

The tardy twosome roared up, decked out in blue, complaining of trouble with a florist. Nevertheless, the boat was festooned with dyed blue flowers, blue net puffballs and other assorted froufrou. The groom told the chaplain that they had tried to get the Don Ho version of the *Hawaiian Wedding Song*, but all they could find was the one by Elvis Presley. The bride flung a fit when, because of a rotten dock, she had to be hopped over a hole in her long blue gown.

But after a bit more confusion, the boat was putt-putting toward the cove. Well, it putt-putted momentarily. Grumbling, the pilot admitted that he had never operated such a boat, so they tediously drifted to the designated site.

Meanwhile, the chaplain was steaming – from the heat, the blue dress, the circumstances and especially over the Elvis music. She thought of her fine educational training and liturgical background, of the three hours of counseling, the two-hour trip the night before and this entire Saturday afternoon and wondered how much all that would be worth.

To her, the whole affair was "tacky, tacky, tacky," but she performed her part just as they had planned. No thanks did she get. But, as she was turning to leave, the groom pressed some money into her hand. She opened it to see: $5. Too relieved to complain, she dodged the goats and hurried back to the sanctity and the sanity of the women's college.

Southern Protestants were somewhat taken aback when they attended their first Polish wedding in Pennsylvania. The 2:00 p.m. ceremony was followed by a gala reception.

There, a kissing booth had been set up for the groom. To kiss him, female guests paid a dollar a smooch. Meanwhile, the bride was busy dancing with every man in sight. For that privilege, the male dancers stuffed bills (not necessarily of the one-dollar denomination) into a pouch on her arm.

The festivities went on and on. Women went back for kisses over and over. Men lined up again and again to dance with the bride. It was 2:00 a.m. and many dollars later when the reception came to an end.

At another Polish wedding reception (this one in Illinois), the groom received envelopes containing money or checks with every handshake. He passed some on to his bride and tucked others into his coat pockets.

Before the honeymoon, he stopped by home to change his clothes, leaving his tuxedo to be returned to the rental shop.

You guessed it. No store employee ever admitted seeing any envelopes, much less the cash or checks. Not only was the hapless couple without their wedding booty, but they knew not whom to thank.

The bandleader at the '90s reception in a Northern city insisted on being paid in cash. For that reason, the father-of-the-bride had $5,000 in his inside coat pocket.

As the evening wore on and the music heated up, he took off his coat and draped it on the back of his chair. You guessed it – when he went to pay the band, no money.

Several weeks later, after the bride and groom returned from their honeymoon, the two families gathered to watch videos of the wedding. One camera had been set up to record action at the head table during the reception. The abandoned coat hung on the chair in plain view. A figure appeared, and a hand slipped inside the pocket to remove the cash. There was no doubt who it was: the father of the groom!

Just before the Depression, a minister, when asked his wedding fee responded: "My average is five dollars."

But when a groom handed him a five-dollar bill, he profusely thanked him. "You're the first one to come up to my average!"

"How much do we pay the minister?" is an often-asked question. There is no one answer. But in Presbyterian circles, this is a most important question to the minister's wife. Traditionally, she gets the honorarium.

A retired Presbyterian minister tells three memorable payment incidents in his career:

Even during the Depression, a clergyman in rural Georgia usually could expect twenty to twenty-five dollars from the family planning the nuptials.

In 1931, his little church had no electricity, and the town had no pavement. One day, a deacon called to ask if he and his fiancee could be married in the house where the minister boarded. With permission from the landlady, the minister agreed and assembled two witnesses, the landlady and her maid.

Before leaving, the groom handed the minister an envelope. "Is this enough?" he asked. Inside were three one-dollar bills. Knowing that cotton was not selling and townsfolk were not buying dry goods, the minister nodded.

A soldier stopped the former chaplain on an Atlanta street shortly after World War II. "Chaplain, will you perform my wedding?" He claimed to have been in the minister's regiment. But since it was impossible to know all 3,500 men in it, the chaplain was not sure whether he really was. Nevertheless, he appeared at the time and the address he was given.

Following a simple service on the front porch of a dilapidated house, the soldier stepped up to him with an afterthought:

"Chaplain, you don't charge anything for performing a wedding, do you?"

Probably the most lavish wedding for which he ever officiated was during the 1970s in the largest suburban church he ever served.

Every detail was meticulously planned. Eight or ten bridesmaids wore gorgeous, expensive dresses. The elegant reception was to be at the country club in a city with many private clubs. The parents of the bride even invited a former minister back to participate in the ceremony.

But neither he, nor the former minister, who had traveled at his own expense, were given a dime.

Receptions

Receptions are supposed to be celebrations of the marriage. Sometimes, certain people do not quite have the appropriate "spirit" of the occasion.

Though the reception was only a small gathering of friends at a mammoth Florida home, the liquor ran out before the party was over. The hostess's father, a judge, was out-of-town. No one knows whether he would have approved of mixed drinks being served in his house during Prohibition, but his daughter was determined that the reception would not be a "dry" one. She dispatched two male guests to hasten to the nearest bootlegger to replenish the supply.

"Hasten" perhaps is too mild to describe the way the driver careened through the city streets to and from the "hootch" dealer. A motorcycle cop thought so and pulled them over. "What's the hurry? Going to a fire?"

"No, to a wedding reception at Judge Jackson's house. We ran out of booze, so we went to get some more," replied the driver. "See, there it is." The officer peered at the floor of the back seat where the gallon jar sat.

"Come with me," he instructed, remounting his cycle and waving them forward. A moment or two later, he motioned for another policeman to join the caravan. He led them directly to the neighborhood, through the gates of the judge's mansion, up the driveway and to the door of the house.

At about 3:00 a.m., the party-goers departed, but not before setting the drunk policemen up against two palmettos, one on each side of the driveway, like rag-doll sentinels.

67

Also during the '60s, an usher contended that no one really paid any attention to all the polite words and compliments passed on by the guests to the bride, groom, both sets of parents, maid-of-honor, bridesmaids and other sundry people likely to be standing in the receiving line.

To prove his point, he tried an experiment. He stuck out his hand, smiled, and in a low but audible voice said to the first one in line, "My grandmother died today."

Nodding and smiling, he continued down the row of nodding and smiling people, repeating to each one, "My grandmother died today." No one, not one person, offered condolences.

Certainly the most memorable reception of my lifetime was that of a college roommate. Soon after we arrived in the fellowship hall, I reacted to a commotion behind me. There was my brand new husband wrestling with my roommate on the floor! She was screaming, and everyone else was gaping.

What was happening? What was Randy doing? Had he gone berserk? Other people began screaming, too.

My shock finally subsided, when they were able to explain. After slicing a piece of cake, the bride had turned to feed it to her mate. Her short tulle veil caught the flame of a candle. All eyes were on their mouths. Only my husband saw the fire. He tried to jerk the veil from her head, but the cap was firmly affixed with bobby pins. Instead, she was jolted to the floor, and he jumped atop her, banging at the flames until they were out.

At receptions in the rural South, it is customary to have not only a beflowered white wedding cake, which is often of the angel food variety, but also a groom's cake.

What kind? Devil's food. No one can explain the significance of that symbolism. But bakers say that the chocolate cake frequently is the most popular.

At a reception held on a beach, the cake was in the shape of a sandcastle.

This cake tops them all! At a 1978 reception in Washington, D.C., the elaborate wedding cake was actually ten pudding-cake tiers. The base was a three-level electric fountain surrounded by five slender white plastic columns on which the first two tiers rested. Above that were four plastic Cupids dancing beneath the third tier. On that were the bride and groom figurines under a floral arch and inside four more columns.

Atop those smaller columns was a fourth tier. Two white doves holding a wedding band were perched a foot above eye-level on a pedestal which rose from that top tier.

But that was only part of the culinary masterpiece, which was baked using seven recipes and decorated with icing flowers in a rainbow of colors. For, from tier No. 2, a pair of stairways fanned down to tiers 5 and 6. Stationed along the stairs to the left were four bridesmaid statuettes. The first had a blue gown; the others wore pink, green and yellow. A fifth bridesmaid was poised on tier 5.

Likewise, four groomsmen descended the right stairway to tier 6, where the fifth one waited. Tiers 5 and 6 were on top of more plastic columns extending up from tiers 7 and 8.

These tiers were placed on the table a little less than a foot from the fountain. A cupid danced in the center of each. Four more bridesmaids and four groomsmen descended a second set of white stairways down to tiers 9 and 10 (also on the table), where they were met by the maid-of-honor, best man, two ushers, ring bearer, acolyte and flower girl. Two junior bridesmaids in pink stood on a connecting bridge between tiers 9 and 10 in front of the fountain.

Yes, 27 attendants witnessed this wedding!

Gardenias were supposed to be floating in the fountain. But just before the reception, when the water was turned on, the flow beat down and sunk $500 worth of pretty flowers.

What began as a lovely reception in a fireman's hall in New Jersey turned into to a brawl, when the feud between Romeo's and Juliet's families became a free-for-all. Two hundred guests chose up sides and joined the foray, knocking over chairs, pulling down draperies and breaking windows. It took 60 police officers to restore order. One person was hospitalized, and the bride's uncle was arrested for "defiant trespassing."

This reception was a champagne breakfast at 6:00 a.m., following a spring sunrise wedding at a lake. While the guests contemplated the beauty of the sun's rays spotlighting dogwood blossoms in the woods, the bride, groom and minister were posing for pictures at the end of an old fishing pier. Suddenly the pier creaked under their weight, dropped and flipped all three backwards into the cold lake.

That cowbell chain was tight around the groom's neck. The lock was case-hardened. The reception was disrupted first by the ushers who had locked it on him and thrown away the key. Getting it off then became quite a show. The bride's father, a massive man, proposed to sever the chain with a three-foot bolt cutter. He tried to position the chain and the cutter so that he wouldn't risk decapitating his new son-in-law. Spectators cheered him on. At last, he and a male delegation retired to the pastor's study, where they stretched the groom on the floor. With all his muscles, the father strained and struggled until it snapped free.

This particular family was hot-blooded and hot-tongued.

No one seemed to know what caused the fist fight among two men at the reception, but suddenly, there they were on the dance floor, slugging it out. The band leader, having been in this predicament at another party, tried what had worked the time before. He picked up the tempo and the volume. That turned the two-man fight into a multi-man brawl.

Out of the crowd stepped an older gentleman, taller and larger than the rest. He pulled the two melee-starters apart. One of them slammed him hard on the jaw. The gray-haired hulk did not flinch. With one blow, he sent his assailant sailing over two tables.

Needless to say, that broke up the fight – and the reception.

Near the end of the reception, the ushers stood ready to catch the garter, while a crowd gathered around. When the groom reached under his bride's skirt for her garter, he sneakily transferred an item from his pocket and ceremoniously whipped out the largest pair of panties available from the discount store.

An uninvited guest caused quite a stir at a large reception, when he ran up a white tablecloth. It was clear that either the other guests or the mouse would have to be evacuated. In the flurry of excitement, the mouse got out first.

Two very tall and extremely thin young people were married. The bride's family had nicknamed them "String" and "Bean." After the reception, nobody threw rice. They tossed green beans.

Pesky Pranks

Couples who run away to get married don't know what they're missing. Or do they?

Groom Dale had a bad habit of tying sardines onto the car motors of other wedding couples and undoubtedly expected the worst. So cautious was he about his own auto that he arrived at the church by cab. His plan was to borrow his brother's car after the reception. He would pick up his new wife at her house, where she would be dressing for their trip.

But someone had spotted the brother's car and blocked it. Decorated it, too. Delayed him for a while.

To get away, Dale recklessly bumped the offending "blocker" vehicle. Nothing serious. Just another delay.

A friend, whom we'll call Jimmy, hightailed it to the bride's home to announce that Dale had had a minor accident and wanted Jimmy to bring her to him. She joined Jimmy for a 45-minute circuitous ride around town.

Meanwhile, Dale arrived at his in-laws' home to get his spouse. Upon learning that Jimmy was the culprit, he sped to Jimmy's wife's workplace. Her ears did not want to hear what he had to yell. Totally innocent because she had to work and couldn't even attend the wedding, she had no idea where Jimmy and Dale's bride were.

Her boss tried to calm Dale by saying, "You may think this is real traumatic today, but ten years from now, you may wish you'd never found her." That did not do the trick.

An hour after the car-crunching, Jimmy returned the kidnapped bride to the arms of her fuming groom.

No dainty tinkling necklace was the family's cowbell which hung around the groom's neck. The bride's brothers, pranksters all, had affixed it with lock and key.

No one in that small West Virginia town in the late 1940s would help him get it off – not during the rehearsal dinner, not anytime during the wedding day, not even after the reception. The huge, ugly bell still clanked when the couple went on their honeymoon. Only when they got to another city could the unfortunate guy get assistance from a stranger and relief from the clangor.

Mischievous ushers surrounded Randy and me, as we hustled toward the door of the church amid showers of rice. Someone snapped something around my wrist that also held the strap to the round hatbox of my luggage set. Suddenly, we realized they had cinched us with handcuffs, my right wrist to his left. But I was on his right side, so our arms were locked in front of us. The heavy hatbox banged awkwardly against my going-away suit, while we ran to the car. Randy couldn't drive! No way could he steer with luggage in his lap.

An obliging cousin hopped behind the wheel. Someone yelled, "If you want the key, join the party at Don's." Only as a last resort would we spend even a part of our wedding night at a party. So Randy gave my cousin directions to the downtown police station. Car after car caravaned behind us, honking all the way into the police driveway. Randy and I jumped clumsily out and into the station.

A cop with a master key was summoned. "Don't worry," he assured. "This key works on 95 percent of all cuffs."

Ours, obviously, was among the other 5%. No wonder. They were Spanish shackles! The law enforcement officer shook his head.

Another policeman with keys was called in. And another. Finally, we were free, much to the disappointment of our pursuers.

An insurance company executive remembers putting "foot cuffs" on a fraternity brother:

"Yeah, he came out of the church dressed for his honeymoon, and I was sitting about halfway down the stairs," the insurance man said. "When his feet got in front of me, I snapped a pair of handcuffs around his ankles." "How did he get out?"

"I don't know. I didn't have a key and didn't see him after that. I canceled his honeymoon reservations, too. He never spoke to me again."

Just about everyone finds their getaway car decorated. Most honeymooners get rice in their car. A couple from Charleston, South Carolina, got 100 crickets. As they sped down the highway in the dark, all 100 chorused a screeching lullaby. The groom halted the car, so that they could open the doors and release their stowaways. Few left. Even after a thorough cleaning at a car wash the next day, several of the critters chirped "good luck" for the rest of their honeymoon.

"Did anyone play a prank on you?" I asked.

"No, 'cause I was too busy playing pranks on them," responded a young man, who had been married about a dozen years. He chuckled. "The ushers hunted all day for my car. Even at the end of our reception at the country club, they were still searching in the parking lot, when the helicopter landed on the lawn and swooped us up."

A mischievous grin tilted his lips. "I rented Snoopy, the police 'copter," he snickered. "And I bombarded them with rice."

"My wife was holding on to my waist, and I was leaning out throwing rice. I can still see a woman who was quite large in a big blue dress and blue hat, looking up and yelling, 'He's gonna fall out! He's gonna fall out!'"

The brother of the groom rolled under the groom's car in his tuxedo to pull the ignition wires. That had not been the original plan, but his brother, wary of pranks, had locked the hood.

Grumbling, the groom later opened the hood and reached in to repair the damage. Not only did he resent the delay, but he didn't want to dirty his new suit.

"I'll fix it," offered the tricky-turned-helpful brother, who reconnected the wires.

Grateful that his brother had made the repairs, the groom grabbed his bride, hopped into the car and "scratched off" out of the driveway. Just a short way down the road, his motor choked and died.

That gallant brother of his had gone back to Plan A, when he was under the hood. He had clamped the gas line.

The bride and groom knelt in the chancel to pray. Snickers and stirring from the congregation behind them diverted the bride. She kept glancing over her shoulder to see what was going on back there. Later, she discovered that, on the bottom of her husband's shoes were the words "Help me!"

Now, from all indications, this was not an unusual prank played by ushers especially during the '40s and '50s. But this was the '80s, and the jokester was the groom.

Another variation: on the bride's soles were "H" and "E;" on the groom's, "L" and "P."

Several days before the wedding, a package came in the mail to the bride. It was postmarked from the state where her husband-to-be, a naval officer, was stationed. Inside was a strange key and a note: "This may be the key to the whole situation." She had no idea what it was.

Her 36-year-old fiance could have used that key. At a bachelor party, his navy buddies had locked a heavy ball and chain on his ankle. He had to bump it up the steps to his apartment and sleep with it until he could locate someone to cut it off.

This poor groom got the ball-and-chain trick played on him the night before his wedding. Unlike his country friends, the city boy had considerable trouble finding someone with a hacksaw to release him. Only one hour before the service did he get free.

That same fellow had to unstuff a front seat full of balled up newspapers before he and his bride could get away. They didn't take time to unstuff the back seat. Forty miles down the road, the newspapers began moving, and up popped an usher with a pad and pencil. He had been recording everything said by the newlyweds. Exasperated, the groom threw him out on the road and sped away.

To the groom's car, model airplane enthusiasts attached a servo switch (a mechanism used to control the throttle of a model plane) to activate the horn. Behind the racing getaway car, the pranksters followed with their radio controls, honking the groom's horn at will, mile after mile after mile.

At a country wedding on a hot July afternoon, the bride and groom were sweltering. The ascot worn by the groom was wet, and the bride, like the groom, was perspiring. Both were relieved when it was time to head for the car. In honor of the groom, who had taken about all the ribbing he could stand for his Alabama accent, grits rained on their heads. Huge handfuls of grits sprinkled on their clothes and splattered and stuck on their faces. They jumped into the car, started off in a rush and got away from the well-wishers.

"Turn on the air-conditioning," the bride sighed.

Whoosh! Clouds of grits whizzed at them from every vent and clung to every bead of perspiration.

Years later, when the car was sold, it was still "gritty."

Sardines were attached to the manifold of the groom's pride-and-joy, a yellow GTO. The stench was nauseating. When he and his bride returned from their honeymoon, they had to trade the car.

Some ushers don't care whether they see the results of their trick. Hearing about it, or imagining, is enough for those who do such devilment as greasing the toilet seat in the bride's dressing area with Jergen's lotion. Reportedly, that causes someone with a small build to "fall in."

Frankly, I can imagine a "falling out" over that one.

How about these pesky pranks:

• Tincture of violet painted from the waist down on the groom, a "decorated" gift for the bride.

• The groom's pajamas sewn across each leg, so that his foot would not go farther than Bermuda-shorts length.

• Rice in the bride's makeup. An unpleasant, expensive mess.

• Talcum powder on the kneeling bench. After the prayer, the groom's trousers had attention-getting white streaks.

• Empty luggage packed in the getaway car. The couple had to make a five-hour return trip to retrieve their clothes.

• A heavy chain wrapped around and around the groom and padlocked during the reception. A photo-spoiler.

• "Just married" written inside the gas cap, so service station attendants would puzzle the honeymooners by congratulating them. An oft-repeated occurrence.

• Watermelon rinds under the front tires of the groom's car, making the wheels to spin in place.

• Rotten shrimp in hubcaps, giving the entire car an unforgettable "perfume."

• Vaseline writing on the car exterior, unnoticed until one hundred miles down the road, when dirt and dust began adhering to the words and designs.

• Paper rose petals stuffed behind the car's sunvisors to "shower" the couple on a sunny day.

First Night

A couple's wedding night should be the most romantic of their entire lives. It doesn't always work out that way.

To foil his pursuers, a groom had paid a farm hand in advance to drive his tractor across the entrance to their farm. The worker was to let them in and keep everyone else out. But the farm worker took the ten bucks to the liquor store before his boss and new bride returned from the church.

The "just married" car appeared from around a bend, with vehicle after vehicle in hot pursuit. Dutifully, the drunk farmhand putt-putted his tractor *in front* of the getaway car! And those rude groomsmen kept the couple up all night.

The groom's uncles had a history of practical joke-playing at weddings. He probably thought he had gotten off easy, when he drove off with his bride for their honeymoon. But one uncle, a dentist, had deliberately put his black bag of professional "tools of the trade" into the couple's car. Later, the culprit called the Highway Patrol to report the bag stolen.

In some little unfamiliar town, the groom was thrown in the "clink," and the bride was put up in a motel for the night. No doubt, she had doubts about the family she was marrying into. Finally, the groom's mother, upon hearing of the joke, grew hysterical and insisted that the uncle undo his mischief.

That was 25 years ago, and none of the family can yet speak civilly about the incident.

In a similar tale, the "stolen" item was the Cadillac loaned to the groom by his boss. When the boss denied knowing the "thief," the groom spent their first honeymoon night in jail. But this bride, at least, could return to her parent's home until morning.

A knock on the hotel room door started the honeymooners' first night as man and wife. Grabbing a towel to go around his waist, the groom opened the door - to a belly dancer in mini-regalia.

"In there or out here?" she politely asked before beginning the show.

"Uh, out here," he said, stepping into the hall to join the eight or ten other amused gawkers. On went the tape and round and round went the exotic dancer's hips (and everything else) to the rhythm.

The bride peered through a crack in the doorway, convinced that her show inside was far superior.

Her father, who had a hotel business in Virginia, had arranged for the honeymooners to stay in the elegant Grove Park Inn in Asheville, N.C.

That was in the late '50s, when a bride's going-away outfit traditionally included a hat. She took off her hat before entering the Grove Park, so that no one would guess they were honeymooners.

She might as well have worn it, for as she and her husband entered the lobby, the staff and guests broke out in song, "Here comes the bride, all dressed in white. Here comes the groom with his britches too tight."

On the very first day of their honeymoon at a South Carolina beach, both bride and groom got severely sunburned – so burned that they had to sleep in separate beds all week.

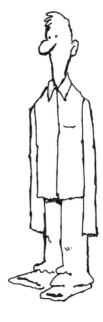

The bride had a surprise for her beloved on their wedding night in the 1920s: white pajamas with blue piping to match hers which had pink piping. Truth was, she was afraid he didn't own any.

As her boyfriend had always seemed a giant to her, she had bought the largest size she could find.

She will always remember him standing in the middle of the hotel room, with cuffs spread out on the floor and sleeves dangling. "I think they're a little too big," he said.

The bridegroom was dejected. His car needed major repairs, and he couldn't pay for those and take a honeymoon, too. Not to worry. His best buddy came to the rescue.

"I'm not one to loan out my car," explained the buddy ten years later. "So I took 'em to Myrtle Beach and stayed with them."

"In the same room?"

"Yep. The first night, he and I got in the same bed, and we told her to get in the other one."

"Surely..."

"She didn't like that much. She wouldn't hear of it." He snickered. "So I kept making noises all night razzin' them."

"Did you stay all weekend?"

"Sure. But the next night, she locked the door, and I had to sleep out in the car."

This poor bride and groom spent their first few nights together in a local motel. Their "real" honeymoon was spoiled by the bride's case of hemorrhoids. She had to stay in town for medical treatment.

When friends rented the room above the honeymooners' motel suite, the couple got in trouble. They beat the ceiling so hard to make their pals shut up that they knocked a hole in the plasterboard.

As they were leaving for their honeymoon, someone handed the bride and groom a "goodie box" with food from the reception. This was a traditional gesture in the '60s, a little something to go with the champagne in the bridal suite.

Only the groom's friends had added a few more "little somethings" to the box: tiny white mice – *live* ones.

On the morning after their "first night," a couple awoke and rolled out of the motel bed. Simultaneously, two of the Texas A & M graduate's fraternity brothers rolled out from under the bed.

Many other interviews about first nights inferred that tricks were quite common. Tricks like these:

• Cancelled reservations. Numerous couples reported this one.

• Short-sheeted bed, "decorations" and a sink full of ice and champagne in the bridal chamber.

• All-night visits by supposed-friends in the couple's hotel room.

• Room service deliveries all through the night. In one instance, it was a tray of glasses and a pitcher of iced tea.

• Constant phone calls, with callers asking what they were doing.

• An invasion of the hotel room after the luggage was deposited but before the couple arrived. The invaders poured rice into pillowcases, put shaving cream into undies and stole all the room's light bulbs and the bride's birth control pills.

Oh, By The Way...

Quite a few weddings do not end with the reception.

New to town, the young minister was lying on his den sofa watching a football game, when his six-year-old son rushed into the room.

"Daddy, have you got a wedding today?" he asked with a hint of alarm.

"No, son."

"Well, there's a lady getting out of a car with a long white dress on!" The little boy had been looking out the manse window toward the church next door.

The minister jumped up and rushed outside in his Bermuda shorts. Sure enough, there was a bride, bridesmaids, ushers, etc. in their finery, gathering in front of the church. Perturbed, he hurried toward them.

They laughed and explained that the mother-of-the-bride had been critically ill and could not attend the wedding held two months earlier. For her, the wedding party had dressed up and reassembled for photos that would include the one who had been absent.

"Is this you, dearie?" The somewhat elderly lady held up a newspaper clipping with my picture, as my new husband and I were seating ourselves on the plane. We were headed to Miami the morning after our wedding.

My eyes bulged comic-book-style, as I glanced at my announcement and the stranger's face. My chin dropped when she added, patting her husband's arm, "We went to your wedding."

Stunned, I could not stop staring, until she explained. "I'm Sarah's aunt from Florida."

Ah, hah. Sarah, my across-the-street neighbor was married at the very same hour at Myers Park Baptist Church on a triangular corner only two blocks away from our church, Myers Park United Methodist, on another triangular corner.

All month, stores had been misdelivering gifts to the wrong bride's house. But, until then, I had not connected our shared wedding date to another incident which had occurred when my father and I were poised at the top of the aisle. "Hurry up!" he had warned. "They're already leaving."

Sarah's aunt and uncle from Florida discovered they had entered the wrong church only when they did not recognize the bride.

The groom was 82; his bride in her 60s. Their wedding day dawned to reveal ten inches of snow on the ground.

The minister called to offer to pick them up in his four-wheel drive vehicle, but the groom declined.

He and his gal arrived on time for their noon wedding in the church chapel. But where did they go next? To a reception? A honeymoon? Nope. The groom drove his new bride to the beauty parlor, so that she could keep her postponed hair appointment.

When this affluent, somewhat conceited family in the Philippines proudly played back the video from their daughter's wedding, they were dismayed at what they saw. The cameraman's video eye had strayed from the main characters to record zoom-ins of certain guests picking their noses and scratching parts of their bodies.

The superior court judge read about it in what was North Carolina's largest newspaper during the 1950s. In a mountain resort town, a fashionable wedding had been held which drew dignitaries from throughout the area. He took special note of a newspaper photo of the bride and groom, leaving in an antique hansom cab. A portly member of the state legislature was smiling from the high driver's seat. The judge was particularly surprised to see that another superior court judge had officiated at the wedding.

A few days later, he was in Raleigh and stopped by to see the Chief Justice. "Has the legislature changed the law to empower a superior court judge to marry people?" he asked. The answer was "no."

The judge wrote his colleague a polite note mentioning that fact. Apparently, his revelation was not appreciated, for he has never to this day heard from the man again.

But the portly legislator called him within a week to verify the Chief Justice's statement. "In that case, what should the couple do?" the legislator wanted to know, when convinced of the seriousness of the situation.

"Tell them not to do anything until it's legal," the judge advised.

"I can't. They're on a cruise to Europe."

The whistle-blowing judge never heard whether the ship's captain validated that marriage.

An eligible bachelor for years, the son of a North Carolina judge had finally married and, on his wedding day, stopped in Charlotte to introduce his bride to his cousin. He said the clerk of court in Rowan County had married them a few hours before.

"The clerk of court? I never heard of a clerk of court conducting a wedding," commented the cousin, who was also a judge.

"She said that, too," replied the groom. "But I reminded her that the Wilkes County clerk of court has been doing it for years. She said "Okay, if that is so.'"

Intrigued, the judge telephoned a fellow judge in Raleigh. At the end of their conversation, the judge put down the phone and grinned. "The clerk of court in Wilkes County is a Primitive Baptist preacher. He was doing it as an ordained minister. Better go back to Rowan County, retrieve those papers and find a justice of the peace."

Early in the week after a Saturday wedding in the '50s, the church secretary noticed on the papers she was mailing to the court that the couple had purchased their marriage license in another county. In their state, the ceremony had to be in the same county where the license was bought.

She notified the preacher, who notified the best man that the marriage was not legal.

Much to the embarrassment of all involved, the preacher had to rush over to the other county the very day they returned from their honeymoon to remarry them.

At the Friday night rehearsal, an Oklahoma minister discovered that the couple's license was not valid for the county where the church was located. Of course, all county offices were closed for the weekend.

What did they do? They went on with the formal ceremony "for show" on Saturday night. Later, the minister traveled with them across the county line and married them in their car.

Don't ask whether there were witnesses.

Also in Oklahoma, a couple realized two months after they were wed that their marriage was not legal because the license was bought in the wrong county. They had not been getting along well and the "wife" refused to remarry her "husband."